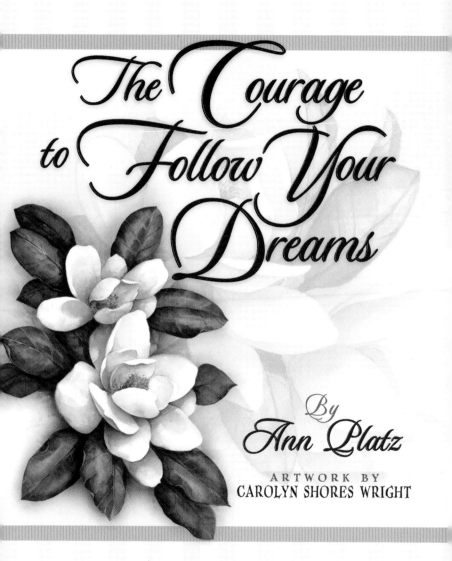

The Courage to Follow Your Dreams

By Ann Platz

ARTWORK BY
CAROLYN SHORES WRIGHT

HARVEST HOUSE PUBLISHERS
Eugene, Oregon

The Courage to Follow Your Dreams

Text Copyright © 2001 by Ann Platz
Published by Harvest House Publishers
Eugene, Oregon 97402

Library of Congress Cataloging –in-Publication Data

Platz, Ann.
   The courage to follow your dreams / Ann Platz; artwork by Carolyn Shores
Wright.
                p. cm.
      ISBN 0-7369-0561-8
         1. Women—Religious life. 2. Courage—Religious aspects—Christianity.
         3. Flowers—Religious aspects—Christianity. I. Title.

   BV4527.P62 2001
   242'.643—dc21

                                                2001016951

Artwork designs are reproduced under license from © Arts Uniq' ®, Inc.,
Cookeville, TN and may not be reproduced without permission. For more
information regarding art prints featured in this book, please contact:

         Arts Uniq'
         P.O. Box 3085
         Cookeville, TN 38502
         1.800.223.5020

Design and production by Garborg Design Works, Minneapolis, Minnesota

Harvest House Publishers has made every effort to trace the ownership of
all poems and quotes. In the event of a question arising from the use of a
poem or quote, we regret any error made and will be pleased to make the
necessary correction in future editions of this book.

Scripture quotations are from the New King James Version of the Bible.
Copyright © 1982 by Thomas Nelson, Inc. Used by permission. All rights
reserved.

Printed in Hong Kong.

01 02 03 04 05 06 07 08 09 10 / NG / 10 9 8 7 6 5 4 3 2 1

TO MY DAUGHTERS

Courtney Cloer Norton

AND

Margaret Fitzgerald Cloer

May you both be powerful women
of courage and
may your lives be full and rich.
Do not fear adversity.
Learn to gain wisdom through
the discovery of who you are and the world around you.

ACKNOWLEDGMENTS

Thank you, all the staff at Harvest House Publishers, for the privilege of writing this book. I especially thank Barb Sherrill and her staff.

To Anne Severance, my editor, you are precious and priceless to me.

To Melissa Woolery and Fran Beaver, thank you for your expert help.

To John Platz, my beloved husband, thank you never seems adequate...I love you.

To my family and friends, you add so much love and comfort. Thank you.

Introduction

No matter where my travels may take me, I always marvel at the fine architecture of centuries past, the imprint of ancient civilizations. But it is in the fabulous gardens of the world that flowers speak a universal language. Season by season, living things reveal lessons of courage, endurance, strength, and loveliness.

Words have similar power. "A word fitly spoken is like apples of gold in pictures of silver," wrote Solomon in the Book of Proverbs. This book attempts to capture the aroma of truth spoken by the flowers and frame them in "pictures of silver."

Each "picture" is presented in bold brushstrokes. "The Flower" reveals the botanical name of the plant and characteristics of its growth and care. "The Fruit," taken from many books on the Victorian language of flowers, defines the virtues and traits symbolized by each flower. "Woman of Courage" identifies a person who best personifies that virtue.

Finally, dear reader, "The Fragrance" is addressed to you, encouraging you to live in such a way that the mingled bouquet of dignity, strength, love, hope, innocence, and purity will perfume and change your world.

Ann Platz

TABLE OF CONTENTS

Aster

(COMPOSITAE)
TINY BEGINNINGS

Despise not the day of small beginnings.
THE BOOK OF ZECHARIAH

THE FLOWER...ASTER

A dainty, star-shaped flower, the aster blooms in autumn, keeping company with its cousin, the bold chrysanthemum. The petals—pink, purple, lavender, or red—fan out from bright golden centers like clusters of stars in the night sky. These blossoms are marvelous both in floral arrangements and in outdoor plantings, preferring full sunlight and plenty of moisture in the garden.

In Britain, the aster was later renamed "Michaelmas daisy" in honor of the feast of St. Michael, which occurred at the peak of this flower's bloom cycle. Asters appear as showers of brilliantly colored stars, enhancing any setting or occasion.

For man, autumn is a time of harvest, of gathering together.
For nature, it is a time of sowing, of scattering abroad.
EDWIN WAY TEALE

THE FRUIT...BEGINNINGS

How interesting that Michaelmas, a traditional British feast day and the namesake of the Michaelmas daisy, was a time of beginnings: the launch of the academic year at Oxford and Cambridge, the opening of the quarterly court session, the day for debts to be settled and annual rents to be paid.

Yet beginnings are often quite simple and small. Who would suspect that a tiny acorn contains a mighty oak? Or that two microscopic cells can unite to form a living being within the human body? Or that great accomplishments begin with great expectations?

The woman of small beginnings must have the courage to live without limits. She must recognize that pain and rejection are a part of growth toward great- ness. She must under- stand that beginnings, no matter how hum- ble, are the origins of dreams, the incep- tion of destiny.

Mighty things from small beginnings grow.
JOHN DRYDEN

Woman of Courage...

Mary, Mother of Jesus

Have you ever wondered why God chose a simple peasant girl, probably no more than 14 or 15 years of age, to participate in a miraculous birth that would change all of history? What courage was required for her to believe the angel's message, announcing that she would be the mother of the Christ child.

It was a star, shaped like the aster and shining more brightly than any other on the night Mary's Son was born, that led shepherds and kings to His birthplace—a stable, a simple stall, a crude manger filled with hay. What humble beginnings. What a surprise to find God in human flesh!

As the brilliant, full-bloomed aster springs from a tiny seed, so

Thus out of small beginnings
greater things have been
produced by His hand that
made all things of nothing, and
gives being to all things that are.
WILLIAM BRADFORD

Mary's womb cradled a King. And like that starflower, which blooms bravely in the face of impending winter knowing that spring will follow, Mary's Son, the One who created the stars, faced His own death with the full assurance of resurrection.

THE FRAGRANCE

Woman of courage,
do not be afraid to sow seed into the soil of your life.
Nurture your faith. Bathe it in the waters of kindness.
May it flourish in the Son-light.
Seeds of greatness will then spring up to maturity
to bless those who breathe in your fragrance.

TINY BEGINNINGS ARE BIRTHINGS.
TINY BEGINNINGS ARE DAWNINGS.
TINY BEGINNINGS ARE THE SEEDS OF GREATNESS.
TINY BEGINNINGS ARE THE ORIGINS OF DESTINY.

Bluebell

Spring unlocks the flowers to paint the laughing soil.
REGINALD HEBER

THE FLOWER...BLUEBELL

The advent of spring deserves the chiming of bells, a parade, and a party! What better springtime celebration than the birth of the bluebells, carpeting woodland floors with shimmering sheets of color, like a mirror for the sky?

This delicate little flower grows in heavy clusters, bending its stalk as if in the act of ringing its bell-like blossoms. It is a relative of the hyacinth, the Greek valerian, and certain plants of the waterleaf family. But it is never more at home than in the woods where it grows wild, scenting the atmosphere with its subtle sweetness and surprising the woodland wanderer.

Enter these enchanted woods,
you who dare.
GEORGE MEREDITH

THE FRUIT...CONSTANCY

Constancy is another word for steadfastness—sustaining the pace, persisting, keeping on. Those who run with patience receive the prize and deserve the hero's welcome—a ticker tape parade, a celebration, and a time to ring those bells!

The secret of success is constancy to purpose.
BENJAMIN DISRAELI

The woman of constancy is well trained and prepared for the task that lies ahead. She looks past the fleeting or temporary to the enduring. Although the steadfast woman competes only with herself, she runs the race to win. She is willing to catch her second wind and surpass her own expectations.

The steadfast woman knows that this is no time for impatience or pride. She is not in a rush. With perseverance and diligence, she may achieve the unthinkable and, like the surprise of woodland bluebells, find her reward in unexpected places.

Woman of Courage...

Wilma Rudolph

Some would have said that Wilma Rudolph didn't have a chance to win the Olympic gold medal for track and field in 1960. She was African-American, six feet tall, and beautiful.

But Wilma had beaten odds greater than those in the past. When she was young, Wilma contracted polio, which attacks the nervous system and causes muscles to atrophy. A daily battle was waged to strengthen her muscles and restore her body back to health. By overcoming polio, Wilma looked past the fleeting and held tightly onto her dreams. She was not shaken.

THE FRAGRANCE

Woman of courage,
Your steadfast heart will endure to the end
and overcome every obstacle.
As you cross the finish line into the winner's circle,
we applaud your grace, your endurance, and your faith.
May you be surprised by success!

In the final seconds of
the track and field
event in
Rome, she
threw back
her head,
churned her long
legs, and sprinted to
victory. In this effort, one
Olympic historian stated that
Wilma changed the sport for all time—
not only because of her superior athleticism,
but because her beauty and social grace helped set a new
standard for women in sports. As one *New York Times*
reporter wrote, "A woman can be tall and lithe with the
good looks associated with fashion and still run with a
vengeance."

Wait, thou child of hope, for Time shall teach thee all things.
MARTIN FARQUHAR TUPPER

CONSTANCY IS FOCUSED.
CONSTANCY IS QUIET POWER.
CONSTANCY IS UNWAVERING.
CONSTANCY ENDURES TO THE END.

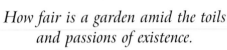

Camellia

(THEACEAE)
EXCELLENCE

*How fair is a garden amid the toils
and passions of existence.*
BENJAMIN DISRAELI

THE FLOWER...CAMELLIA

This lush shrub is most at home in milder climates, such as Southern gardens or greenhouses. It is prized for its thick, dark glossy foliage and lovely dense white blossoms. Cultivated for centuries in China for its leaves—which, when dried and ground, make a fine tea—the specimen finally made its way to the West.

Despite its beauty, the camellia is a stable, no-nonsense plant, loaded with seasonal blooms that last for several weeks. Yet strangely absent is a pleasing scent. Still, even without the mystery of perfume, these are flawless flowers, excellent for showing by horticulturists.

*By a garden is meant mystically a place of
spiritual repose, stillness, peace,
refreshment, delight.*
JOHN HENRY CARDINAL NEWMAN

THE FRUIT...EXCELLENCE

Excellence is that quality of superior achievement to which all aspire but few attain. Yet she who moves in excellence rises above the masses.

The woman of excellence holds herself to a higher level of achievement and accountability. Rather than resting on her laurels, she strives to accomplish more, to be productive, to excel. Her worth lies in her quality of thought as well as in her actions.

A trailblazer and a vision-bearer, the woman of excellence is not bound by self-imposed limitations. Because of her accomplishments, she wields the power and authority to influence others. By stretching and strengthening her vision, the excellent woman sees far beyond the horizon.

Let each teach others
who themselves excel.
ALEXANDER POPE

Woman of Courage...

Golda Meir

Like the camellia with its sturdy, no-nonsense durability, Golda Mabovitch Meir may have appeared somewhat fragile on the outside, but she was tough as nails on the inside. Born in Kiev, Ukraine, she moved with her family to America and taught school in Milwaukee. She later moved to Israel in 1917 and became a masterful fundraiser for the Zionist cause.

In May, 1948, Mrs. Meir was one of the signers of the Israeli Declaration of Independence. She held several high government positions and was eventually named foreign minister. In recognition of her supreme contributions to the State of Israel, she was asked to fill in as Prime Minister after the death of the incumbent in 1969. Later, she was elected in her own right. A strong and skillful negotiator, she is the only woman to hold the

THE FRAGRANCE

Woman of courage,
never be content to rest on your laurels.
The sky is the limit.
Strive passionately to soar above the clouds.
Fix your eyes on the goal and press ahead.
May your excellent work be rewarded
with the satisfaction of a life well lived.

high office of Prime Minister in Israel and remains one of the country's great leaders, "a beloved mother among the founding fathers."

With regard to excellence, it is not enough to know,
we must try to have and use it.
ARISTOTLE

EXCELLENCE SOARS ABOVE THE CLOUDS.
EXCELLENCE CATCHES THE VISION.
EXCELLENCE DOES NOT REST ON ITS LAURELS.
EXCELLENCE IS ITS OWN REWARD.

Carnation

(CARYOPHYLLACEAE)
TO CROWN

It is a golden maxim to cultivate the garden for the nose,
and the eyes will take care of themselves.
ROBERT LOUIS STEVENSON

THE FLOWER...CARNATION

This lovely blossom, resembling a fringed cap cut with pinking shears, was used to make ceremonial crowns in ancient Greece. Thus, its name, some scholars believe, is from the word meaning "coronation." Others seem to think that the name comes from carnis, meaning "flesh," and refers to the Incarnation—"God made flesh." By any definition, the carnation is a "divine flower."

A favorite of kings and noblemen as well as the common folk, you will find this richly scented flower— something like the pungent, spicy-sweet aroma of cloves—in florist shops and gardens alike. In the garden, carnations are more commonly called "pinks" or "Sweet William" (named for William the Conqueror who favored this flower above all others), with the color ranging from pink to red, although white and yellow varieties are also cultivated.

He who reigns within himself and rules his passions, desires, and fears is more than a king.
JOHN MILTON

THE FRUIT...TO CROWN

The act of coronation is an event of great pomp and circumstance. To be crowned is to be set apart for a high calling, to be empowered with rank and privilege. Crowns follow the royal line or are granted as a result of superior service.

The woman of royalty understands her mission and the boundaries of her kingdom. She is equipped to do her duty. Strength and courage are her badges of honor. She holds her head high, pressing toward the goal.

This woman of honor will risk her life for the cause and for others. She will be guided by a greater vision, using nonviolent weapons of spiritual warfare to protect those under her care.

I do not ask for any crown
But that which all may win;
Nor try to conquer any world
Except the one within.
LOUISA MAY ALCOTT

Woman of Courage...
Coretta Scott King

Coretta Scott King is a woman of true courage. When her beloved husband, Martin Luther King, Jr. was martyred for his stand in the Civil Rights Movement, Coretta stepped forward to leadership. Martin and Coretta not only partnered in marriage, but also shared the same world vision—a vision of peace.

During their marriage, Martin often sent Coretta red carnations as a reminder of his love for her when he was away. No matter the distance between them, they stood together in their call to non-violent social change. Little did she know that daily she was being trained for the time when

THE FRAGRANCE

Woman of courage,
the crown requires crucifixion to selfish ambition.
The kingdom within you must be conquered
before you can rule others wisely.
Set noble goals. Move in faith and strength
along the pathway that is set before you,
and you will receive the "crown of life."

the mantle would be passed to her. The red carnations were not only an expression of Martin's love for Coretta, but also a prophetic symbol of her future crowning.

When her husband died, leaving four young children to rear, Coretta not only led the cause, but covered her family as well. The courage and wisdom she displayed, by choosing to continue, rather than succumbing to her grief, proved Coretta Scott King to be a valiant crusader. She carried on her husband's legacy and claimed her destiny as a woman of courage.

A virtuous woman is a crown to her husband.
THE BOOK OF PROVERBS

A CROWN SIGNIFIES AUTHORITY.
A CROWN BESTOWS HONOR.
A CROWN REFLECTS KINGDOM WORK.
A CROWN IS THE REWARD OF EXCELLENCE.

Chrysanthemum

(DENDRANTHEMA)
HOPE

I perhaps owe having become a painter to flowers.
CLAUDE MONET

THE FLOWER...CHRYSANTHEMUM

Once, on a trip to Europe, we visited Monet's garden home, Giverny, just outside Paris. The chrysanthemums were blooming, as if daring the freeze that had been forecast. On the very eve of destruction, the blossoms—copper, orange, deep gold, and brilliant yellow—were at their most glorious.

The last flowers of the season, chrysanthemums seem to defy both cold snaps and Indian summer until, finally, their blooms spent, they succumb to the killing frosts. Winter is coming, but there is a poignant promise in their brilliant colors of fall. Bright and bold as a splash of sunlight on a dreary day, the cheerful chrysanthemum is a harbinger of hope. Its message is emphatic: "Hold on! Don't give up! Better times are ahead!"

Love is the voice under all silences,
the hope, which has no opposite in fear;
the strength so strong mere force is feebleness:
the truth more first than sun,
more last than star...
E.E. CUMMINGS

THE FRUIT...HOPE

The chrysanthemum displays its most vibrant beauty against a backdrop of death and dying. Leaves may finally loosen their tight grip on the branches, and flowers may die, but something is stirring in the air and beneath the surface of the earth. There is more than meets the eye. There is resurrection of life to come.

The woman of hope sees beyond the circumstances. Her faith causes her to rise above her dilemma and to have faith in the unseen. Women who possess this trait inspire others to persevere. Hope challenges the darkness of night. Hope fosters courage and rejects fear. Hope supplies a spirit of courage to rise up within us and reach for the impossible.

Hope springs eternal.
ALEXANDER POPE

Woman of Courage...

Mary Ashley Gardner

My younger sister was only a little past forty when she was first diagnosed with breast cancer. Full of life and vitality, Mary Ashley was like a flower in radiant bloom, lighting up every gathering with her beauty. In fact, flowers were a huge part of her life. It seemed that plants burst into bloom at her touch. She was also known for her exquisite floral arrangements, a gift that she shared freely with friends and family.

Despite her advancing illness and eminent death, Mary Ashley maintained her dynamic optimism, seemingly taking advantage of this opportunity to savor every moment of life, especially with her husband and two-year old son. Her faith was an inspiration to all who knew her—dressing for chemotherapy in cocktail dresses, staging reunions with childhood friends, and inviting dear friends to slumber parties while she was still a patient in the hospital. Life is stronger than death, and Mary Ashley lives on in her legacy of hope and love, bequeathed to those she has left behind.

Live life so completely
that when death comes to you
like a thief in the night,
there will be nothing left
for him to steal.
UNKNOWN

THE FRAGRANCE

Woman of courage,
May hope rise up within you
As you face daily challenges and changes.
Keep pressing on. Never give up!
Obstacles will become teachers,
And you will grow wiser from their lessons.
Hope brings true joy.
May your perfume gladden the hearts that so joyously
share in the abundance of you.

HOPE EXPECTS.
HOPE INSPIRES.
HOPE ENCOURAGES.
HOPE MAKES A PROMISE.

Daffodil

(AMARYLLIDACEAE)
GRACIOUS COURTESY

Daffodils,
That comes before the swallow dares, and takes
The winds of March with beauty.
WILLIAM SHAKESPEARE

THE FLOWER...DAFFODIL

Was there ever a flower like the daffodil, turning its happy face to the sun or catching raindrops in its ruffled cup? An early bloomer, the daffodil heralds the coming of spring and often blooms bravely through late-winter snows. What a bright welcome after the bleakness of that season.

A member of the narcissus family, the daffodil is constructed with a center trumpet that is as long or longer than the surrounding petals—one flower on a single stem. They grow in frilly, lemon yellow drifts wherever they are planted—in random grassy areas or bordering the gardens. Although we expect to find them in every shade of yellow, hybridized versions include white and cream, with pink to orange trumpets.

I wandered lonely as a cloud that floats on high o'er vales and hills,
When all at once I saw a crowd, a host, of golden daffodils.
WILLIAM WORDSWORTH

THE FRUIT...
GRACIOUS COURTESY

As young women, part of our social development is to learn the gracious art of courtesy—consideration, generosity, and grace. Consideration prefers others before yourself; generosity makes ample provision for needs, and grace goes the extra mile, welcoming strangers into your world as warmly as invited guests.

The gracious hostess has been well trained; she gives, not out of a sense of obligation but of love and true hospitality. Her social skills reflect her respect for all people. She is able to make each one feel special and transforms every occasion with her unique touch.

Entering her home, one is greeted with a sense of having been expected, that everything has been prepared for your coming. It is the same sensation of delight that Wordsworth must have experienced when, wandering about one day, he topped a hill and discovered that "host of golden daffodils."

If a [woman] be gracious and courteous to strangers, it shows [she] is a citizen of the world, and that [her] heart is no island cut off from other lands, but a continent that joins to them.
FRANCIS BACON

Woman of Courage...
Jacqueline Kennedy

With the inauguration of John F. Kennedy to the presidency of the United States, worldwide attention was focused on his poised and beautiful young wife. Born to wealth and privilege, the refined Jacqueline Bouvier Kennedy was well prepared for the role of First Lady.

Jacqueline had a deep love for all things beautiful. She brought beauty, grace, and culture to the White House. By seeking the help of distinguished authorities in the area of art and antiques, Jacqueline acquired impressive American antiques and furnishings, and restored dignity to the White House. She renewed an appreciation of our national heritage and through television, welcomed Americans into their national home.

But it was after John Kennedy's assassination that she left the most lasting impression on the heart of America. As a daffodil pushes through the frozen earth to bloom in difficult conditions, so Jackie's finest hour occurred after her husband's death.

We will never forget that brave widow standing with her two small children, just as her little son lifted his hand to give a farewell salute as the funeral cortege passed by.

Her Grace is all she has,
And that, so vast displays,
One Art, to recognize, must be,
Another Art to praise.
EMILY DICKINSON

THE FRAGRANCE

Woman of courage,
just as the daffodil springs forth in the midst of winter,
may you stand tall in seasons of adversity.
Embrace all people.
Warm them in the welcome of your heart.
May you grow strong in your weakest places
and perfume the lives of all who know you.

COURTESY IS CONSIDERATION.
COURTESY IS GENEROSITY.
COURTESY IS PREFERRING OTHERS BEFORE YOURSELF.
COURTESY IS COURTLY BEHAVIOR.

 *Gardenia*

(RUBIACEAE)
GRACE

*Rain is grace; rain is the sky condescending to the earth;
without rain, there would be no life.*
JOHN UPDIKE

THE FLOWER...GARDENIA

In 1754, a British sea captain, strolling along a tropical
shore in South Africa, caught a heavy, sweet scent that
almost took his breath away. Turning, he was astonished to
find masses of fragrant white blooms, as if designed by some
celestial landscape architect. He dug up a shrub and took it
home to London, where it managed to survive before finding a more suitable environment in America's southland.

The gardenia bush blooms for about one month in early
summer. During that short time, the gardenia does not go
unnoticed; its potent and powerful aroma captivates and
enchants everyone who enters the garden. Each stem of the
gardenia bush is heavily laden with lavish ivory blooms,
which are delicate and bruise easily. Just as quickly as the
gardenia blooms, it is gone, leaving the essence of a distinct
aroma, not to be forgotten.

You're only here for a short visit. Don't hurry.
Don't worry. And be sure to smell the flowers
along the way.
WALTER C. HAGEN

THE FRUIT...GRACE

Like the gardenia, the gracious woman exudes a fragrance all her own. Her presence uplifts and inspires those around her. She is like a breath of fresh air, her radiance attracting everyone to her. The secret of her radiance is an unselfish heart. The gracious woman desires to serve rather than to be served. She looks for opportunities to give, to share rich life experiences with others and to find ways to lighten their burdens. The presence of a gracious woman is one of purity and strength. This woman does not go unnoticed.

The woman of grace has an intuitive nature and is sensitive to those around her, although she will be courageous and bold when need be. Her courage will be one of surety of purpose and her life an example of honor. Adversity becomes the agent through which her perfume changes the atmosphere around her, and she considers sacrifice a privilege.

The star that shines twice as bright burns half as long.
AUTHOR UNKNOWN

Women of Courage...

Cassie Bernall and Rachel Scott

When Cassie Bernall and Rachel Scott were faced with the choice between holding to their convictions or denying their faith, they chose to boldly proclaim it. Rather than cower and hide when confronted by two classmates armed with guns, Cassie and Rachel took a courageous stand.

The lives of the two girls were not spared, but they knew in that instant the true meaning of grace. They experienced it. Like an invisible covering, grace provides mercy in the time of need. Grace brings an enveloping peace, which

THE FRAGRANCE

Woman of courage,
your powerful aroma, which is undeniably you,
exudes a message of both toughness and tenderness.
Your name will be forever engraved in the hearts of those
who have experienced your gentle grace
or observed your courageous stand for truth and
righteousness.

roots out fear and brings wisdom and comfort in a time of great anxiety.

These valiant young women proved that courage and conviction have no age limit. Although their lives were gathered while still in the tender bud, their fragrance is like that of the gardenia, leaving a distinct aroma of courage, strength, and grace to move the hearts of those who hear their story.

Earth has no sorrow that heaven cannot heal.
THOMAS MOORE

GRACE IS A DIVINE COVERING.
GRACE IS A GIFT.
GRACE EXTENDS FAVOR.
GRACE IS MERCY.

Gerbera Daisy

(COMPOSITAE)
PURITY

Every flower is a soul blossoming in Nature.
GERARD DE NERVAL

THE FLOWER...GERBERA DAISY

The petals of Gerbera daisies, so evenly spaced, look almost artificial. Add to that the straight, sturdy stem and serrated tongue-like leaves, and you have a picture of near floral perfection.

Loved for their sweet simplicity, daisies come in crayon colors of white, yellow, red, and orange. They flourish in rich soil and bright sunlight, with plenty of water. Once the blossoms have been cut and brought indoors, however, they must be placed upright in a vase, or their heads will begin to droop.

The strongest evidence of love is sacrifice.
CAROLYN FRY

THE FRUIT...PURITY

"Fresh as a daisy!" Remember that old adage? Purity is the state of being fresh and free of dust, dirt, or corruption.

Absent are the contaminants that blemish and soil life. In the purest state, toxic matters have been purged and cleansed, leaving the product clear and clean.

So it is with the woman of purity. Her heart is pure. Her motives are true to the core and do not reflect a personal agenda. Because of her honest transparency, she is able to affect people greatly. The pure woman has been purged of the deception and seduction of the world. She will not be led astray. By giving no place to fear and defeat, she chooses to live courageously, leading others by her example of love, devotion and purpose. The pure woman is a vessel of honor.

No man or woman can be strong, gentle, pure, and good without the world being better for it.
PHILLIP BROOKS

Woman of Courage...

Mother Teresa

She was just a little slip of a thing—this woman whose vows of purity and poverty were made not to a man but to God. Even while she was living, she was regarded as one of the world's most admired and courageous saints.

Agnes Gonxha Bojaxhiu, later known as Mother Teresa, was born to an affluent family in Albania, where she was a fun-loving and mischievous child, without a care in the world. She later confounded everyone by joining a Catholic order of nuns and accepting an assignment to Calcutta, India. There she lived on the streets in the most wretched of conditions, ministering to the poorest of the poor, many of them lepers and persons infected with AIDS. In each suffering face, she saw the dignity of human life.

It was her great respect for life that drove her to demonstrate compassion and charity to all. Like Mother Teresa herself, the order she founded during her years of service is dedicated to the alleviation of human suffering.

The loneliest, the most wretched and the dying have at her hands received compassion without condescension, based on reverence for man.

NOBEL PEACE PRIZE COMMITTEE

THE FRAGRANCE

Woman of courage,
may your life reflect transparency, truth, and honesty.
By remaining simple, uncomplicated, and pure,
you will get to the heart of all things.
Stand tall. Reach for the sun. Receive refreshment
from the rain.
Never bow your head in defeat, only in submission
to a cause that is greater than yourself.

PURITY IS FRESHNESS.
PURITY IS NOT BEING FLAWLESS, ONLY FORGIVEN.
PURITY IS REFINEMENT IN THE FIRE.
PURITY IS SIMPLICITY.

(LILIACEAE)
INNOCENCE

How splendid in the morning glows the lily.
JAMES ELROY FLECKER

THE FLOWER...LILY

The flower most often associated with the celebration of sacred events is the "Madonna" lily, its pure white trumpet heralding the joyful news of resurrection. It should also come as no surprise that historically, the lily has been the flower chosen in wedding ceremonies to symbolize the innocence of the bride and groom.

The lily is a flower that holds a prominent position in the garden. Its sculptured trumpet shape and elongated stem elevate the lily closer to the sun and sky. The fragrance of the lily varies. While the White Casablanca lily is strongly scented and powerful, the orange and yellow day lilies are not scented and are fragrantly understated. From bold and exotic to pale and pure, these blossoms sanctify weddings, pay respect at funerals, adorn the garden, and grace the home.

The heart that is soonest awake to the flowers
Is always the first to be touch'd by the thorns.
THOMAS MOORE

THE FRUIT...INNOCENCE

Innocence is a purity of heart, a freedom from guilt or blame. The innocent hold a freshness of vision not jaded by previous experiences or prejudices. Women who possess this trait are a breath of fresh air in a culture where innocence is too little prized, too often lost.

With this pure heart comes an acceptance of others as they are. No judgment. No condemnation. Only the innocent can see past the appearance of what *is* to the possibility of what can *be*. Such women have not bought into the world's system of half-truths and flattery.

This woman of innocence is uncorrupted by wickedness and deception. She views life through the unfiltered lenses of truth, honesty and purity, inspiring others to follow her example.

Innocence has nothing to dread.
JEAN RACINE

Woman of Courage...

Anne Frank

The rumbling of the Holocaust did not daunt the young Jewish teenager, Anne Frank, as her family hid from Nazi soldiers for two years in an attic. Her positive attitude during their confinement allowed those around her to enjoy the light of her soul. This innocence of a pure and unspotted spirit, exuded from her quite naturally. Not knowing, she did not therefore anticipate the cruel realities of life and was able to see and expect the best.

All the lilies of the prairie,
When on earth they fade and perish,
Blossom in that heaven above us.
HENRY WADSWORTH LONGFELLOW

"No one will be interested in the unbosoming of a 13-year-old schoolgirl," she wrote in one of the notebooks she would fill during her German-Jewish family's self-imposed exile in occupied Holland. Yet *The Diary of Anne Frank* is probably the single most poignant human document of the Holocaust ever recorded. Contained in these notebooks are all the musings of an adolescent heart, yet untouched by the world.

All of these years later Anne Frank's memory lives on in her work that is now required reading for schoolchildren. Anne's innocent optimism gave off the pungent aroma of a lily to her barren attic room that, in her death, has perfumed the world.

THE FRAGRANCE

Woman of courage,
as your mission unfolds,
your fragrance will draw others into your world.
Speak only the truth. Bring all things into the light.
Your message to the hearts of those you touch
will be a treasure forever.

INNOCENCE IS PURE OF HEART.
INNOCENCE IS CLEAR AND CLEAN.
INNOCENCE IS BLAMELESS.
INNOCENCE IS GUILELESS.

Magnolia

There are persons so radiant,
so genial, so kind, so pleasure-bearing,
that you instinctively feel
in their presence that they do you good,
whose coming into a room is like
the bringing of a lamp there.
HENRY WARD BEECHER

THE FLOWER...MAGNOLIA

Towering high above a lush landscape, creamy waxed blossoms caught in her hair, the stately magnolia is the queen of the garden. Spreading her skirts, she presides in regal splendor over her verdant domain. This elegant tree is the essence of the Old South, where soft summer breezes carry her intoxicating fragrance to perfume many gardens.

Before honor is humility.
THE BOOK OF PROVERBS

At "Willbrook," my childhood home in the Low Country of South Carolina, my gentleman farmer father taught me about the magnolia. He told me that as tall as the

44

magnolia tree was in its reach for heaven, so its roots plunge that deeply into the earth, seeking underground springs. Thus the tree is not affected by drought and can withstand extremes of heat and humidity.

THE FRUIT...DIGNITY

The word dignity reflects the image of excellence, elegance, and appropriateness. It is a cloak of honor and respect to all who wear it. At the core of this virtue is humility. The truly dignified woman is neither overbearing nor dominating, but conveys quiet strength.

A woman of dignity has the confidence to stand in the face of adversity. She is deeply rooted to her family and her faith. Like the giant magnolia tree, she can withstand the droughts of life with grace. This dignified woman has developed strength of character and models a life well lived. Just as the magnolia tree extends its branches to provide shade on a hot summer day, so the woman of dignity provides shelter for those who are in need of comfort and renewal.

Dignity is not negotiable. Dignity is the honor of the family.
VARTAN GREGORIAN

Woman of Courage...

Barbara Bush

Mrs. Bush, wearing her white hair like a crown of splendor, is the epitome of grace and dignity. There was no way of knowing on her wedding day that she was marrying a future president of the United States!

The former First Lady's roots go deep in matters of faith and family. As the mother of six, she has experienced the joys of a large family and endured the tragedy of losing a small child to leukemia. Her love for others is expressed in lifelong acts of compassion, for which she has earned great

THE FRAGRANCE

Woman of courage,
as you increase in age and maturity,
may your embrace expand like the giant magnolias,
and may you attain heights you never dared to dream.
As you reach for heaven, your roots will grow deep,
searching for wisdom in the underground
springs of knowledge.
You will bless those
who seek shelter and comfort in your shade.

respect and admiration. Like the giant magnolia, she opens her arms to all and draws them to her in a gesture of warmth and protection.

No one knows like a woman how to say things that are at once gentle and deep.
VICTOR HUGO

Perhaps Mrs. Bush's finest hour was the day she addressed the graduating class of Wellesley College at their commencement ceremony. She spoke as the mother of our country to her spiritual daughters. Imparting the greatest wisdom an older woman can confer on the younger generation, she shared from her heart: "At the end of your life," she said, "you will never regret not having passed one more test, not winning one more verdict, or not closing one more deal. You will regret time not spent with a husband, a friend, a child, or a parent." What wisdom!

DIGNITY IS QUIET STRENGTH.
DIGNITY IS CONFIDENCE.
DIGNITY IS ELEGANT REFINEMENT.
DIGNITY IS EXCELLENCE.

Morning Glory

(CONVOLVULACEAE)
AFFECTION

*Morning glories…so blue…as though someone had torn
great masses out of a morning sky.*
REGINALD ARKELL

THE FLOWER…MORNING GLORY

My favorite early-morning, wake-up call is the silent
"Trumpet Voluntary" of the morning glory. It opens its bell-
shaped blossoms in blue, white, red, and rose-lavender
while the dew is still on the grass, and heralds the coming
of the day. Our mountain house is even located on Morning
Glory Lane in the Great Smoky Mountains of North
Georgia.

How glorious to see this subtly scented flowering vine
climbing mailboxes and fence posts, tumbling over trellises,
and embracing brick walls and banks! But better breathe in
its beauty early, for this delicate flower wilts in the heat of
the sun.

Full many a glorious morning have I seen.
WILLIAM SHAKESPEARE

THE FRUIT...AFFECTION

Affection is a term used for tender attachment, fondness, and feelings of friendship. It is the love of one sister for another, whether bonded by birth or by mutual benefit.

The affectionate woman cannot help demonstrating her caring heart. It is as much a part of her as the morning glory blossom to the vine. Like that twining vine, she reaches out to draw others in, to include rather than to exclude, to champion rather than to criticize.

The woman of affection opens doors—even if she has to climb through—then paves the way for all others to enter. She is dedicated to the proposition that all men—and women—are created equal.

What actions are the most excellent? Those, certainly, which most powerfully appeal to the great primary human affections.
MATTHEW ARNOLD

Woman of Courage...

Oprah Winfrey

One woman who has entwined herself around the hearts of millions of Americans is a child of obscurity, Oprah Winfrey. Now the reigning queen of daytime television, she was once a product of poverty and racism.

All those who give love, gather love.

ANONYMOUS

From these humble beginnings, Oprah carved a place of distinction for herself through determination, unwillingness to accept defeat, and a genuine care for others. She has chosen to use her voice and popularity as a tool to bring positive change to society and to help all people. By overcoming her own trials in life, she easily identifies and empathizes with people every-where. In turn, they find a sister, a friend, and a mentor. She has now opened up a forum for the voices of people everywhere to be heard and helped.

Oprah Winfrey, heart open wide like the morning glory, invites others to share the warmth of her affection and the joy of her triumph over adversity. Her empathy and outstretched arms have drawn the American public into her warm embrace. As an overcomer, she has opened doors so that others can follow where she has led.

THE FRAGRANCE

Woman of courage,
as a friend to the world,
may you reach out to all who need your touch.
The sincerity of your affection brings life and hope.
As a woman of passion and purpose,
you lead through example, encouraging
others to take the hand of a weaker sister.

AFFECTION IS A TENDER HUG.
AFFECTION IS A COMFORTING SMILE.
AFFECTION IS A LISTENING HEART.
AFFECTION IS AN UNDERSTANDING SPIRIT.

Pansy

(VIOLACEAE)
THOUGHTS

Of all the flowers that come and go
The whole twelve months together,
His little purple pansy brings
Thoughts of the sweetest, saddest things.
MARY BRADLEY

THE FLOWER...PANSY

The pansy is a low-hovering, ground-hugging planting, which produces a marvelous, extravagantly textured bloom. The pansy's personality comes forth in a variety of shades, hues, and tints of color. With interesting markings and the beautiful flush of hot to cool colors, pansies are a distinct and unusual flower.

Although the pansy appears to be a delicate flower, it can brave extremes of temperature, enduring a long, hard winter season. The proper time to plant the pansy is in the autumn season. The harsh temperatures of winter's dormant season prove to be an asset to the pansy. When cold temperatures eventually thaw, and spring's lush blossoms are unveiled, the pansy emerges full and vibrant with large, glorious blooms.

This flower thrives on the cold temperatures of winter, and when not planted during that season, the blooms are not as bountiful or colorful.

> *As a man thinketh in his heart, so is he.*
> THE BOOK OF SOLOMON

THE FRUIT...THOUGHTS

The thinking woman is insightful and reflective. Immersed in thought, she ponders the deeper questions of life. She has the courage to step out of conventional life and to question the very basis of how we conduct ourselves and why. These women motivate others and encourage them to expand their capacity to reason and to see all sides of every issue.

Brilliant thinkers affect generations to come. The choice is how you choose to think. If thoughts are true and good, good fruit will be produced. The thinking woman has the courage to question life and the strength to be her own person.

> *Great men are they who see that spiritual is stronger than any material force, that thoughts rule the world.*
> RALPH WALDO EMERSON

Woman of Courage...

Joy Davidman

Few women could have captured the intellect and ultimately the heart of a man like Dr. C. S. Lewis, the great professor at Oxford University. But Joy Davidman was one of the few. With her sharp wit and candor, she challenged him and won. As he himself writes, he was "surprised by joy."

A teacher affects eternity; he can never tell where his influence stops.
HENRY BROOKS ADAMS

Jewish by birth and atheistic by choice, Joy Davidman was an astute student of life. Like a winter pansy, she endured the cruel winds of adversity—a failed marriage and

THE FRAGRANCE

Woman of courage,
you have chosen to go deeper and wider
to mine treasures others could not see.
With your probing mind, you have charted a journey
we would not have taken.
Thank you for giving us the courage to explore life—
both its undiscovered beauty and its tragedy.

bone cancer—before basking in the springtime of her new-found faith and marriage.

For a brief time, with her cancer in remission, Joy was able to thaw the frozen orthodoxy of her husband's intellectualism and help him connect his brilliant mind with his compassionate heart. Even as she was dying, she restored life, balance, and order to his home, where he and his brother had lived as bachelors, leaving him to reflect and write on the changes she had brought.

THOUGHTS ARE BURIED TREASURE.
THOUGHTS ARE REFLECTIVE.
THOUGHTS ARE TRUTH SEEKING.
THOUGHTS ARE INFLUENTIAL.

Peony

(RANUNCULACEAE)

KEEPS A SECRET

Deep in their roots,
All flowers keep their light.
THEODORE ROETHKE

THE FLOWER...PEONY

In rambling about the countryside, you may discover the remains of an old pioneer homestead, the farm abandoned, the walls crumbling. Yet flowering in this wilderness, in the remnant of a garden, is the flamboyant peony, mute testimony to the family who once tilled this soil. Hardiest of all plants, peonies can live for hundreds of years if undisturbed! Oh, the secrets they could tell....

These large and beautiful blossoms greet spring in banners of pink, white, and shades of red. A relative of the camellia, this bloom—often a double bloom—is ruffled in the center. The foliage forms a low, neat shrub during summer and does not die back in winter.

Nothing is too polished to see the beauty of flowers. Nothing is too rough to be capable of enjoying them.
DANIEL WEBSTER

Although peonies thrive under most any condition, they do appreciate a bit of shade in warmer climates.

THE FRUIT...KEEPS A SECRET

The ability to keep a confidence is a virtue that few attain. This agreement requires trust, loyalty, and an unspoken understanding between two people.

The keeper of secrets is a woman of honor. Her word is her bond. Knowing that she has been chosen and entrusted with something precious, she guards that trust. She seals the treasure in her heart, unjudged and unspoken, until she is permitted to release it.

Worthy of trust, the keeper of secrets provides a safe shelter for those who confide in her.

The human heart has hidden treasures,
In secret kept, in silence sealed.
CHARLOTTE BRONTË

Woman of Courage...

Betty Ford

Although having the capacity to keep a secret entrusted to you by someone else is an admirable virtue, Mrs. Gerald Ford, wife of a president who served only a short term, created a legacy by *telling* secrets!

These secrets were very personal problems. Had Betty Ford kept them to herself, the country might never have known about her breast cancer or her addiction to prescription pain pills and alcohol. In sharing her story, however, she raised public awareness to a new level and perhaps, single-handedly, saved more lives than decades

THE FRAGRANCE

Woman of courage,
may you honor the precious trust
that others place in you,
keeping their confidence.
But may you live in such transparency and integrity
that your own life is an open book.

of public-service campaigns.

After checking herself into a hospital specializing in substance-abuse treat-ment, Mrs. Ford emerged, healed and whole. Four years later, she founded the Betty Ford Center to aid others in obtaining a cure for drug dependency. Like the long-lasting peony, Mrs. Ford's bold and courageous stand will endure through the ages.

A secret ceases to be a secret if it is once confided.
JOSH BILLINGS

A KEEPER OF SECRETS IS DISCREET.
A KEEPER OF SECRETS IS TRUSTWORTHY.
A KEEPER OF SECRETS IS A TRUE FRIEND.
A KEEPER OF SECRETS IS WISE.

Queen Anne's Lace

(DAUCUS CAROTA)
CONFIDENCE

The pleasure of picking a few flowers
and finding the right vase for them is incomparable.
MAY SARTON

THE FLOWER...
QUEEN ANNE'S LACE

Resembling a medieval queen's frilly headdress, this wild flower grows in abundance on both field and roadside, like great drifts of snowy lace. The intricate pattern is reminiscent of the elegant handwork done by fine seamstresses in a time when only the very wealthy could afford such luxuries. Yet this flower grows wild and free, to be enjoyed by all in its natural habitat, or to be picked and displayed.

The airy plant with its fernlike leaf fronds—some have even had the nerve to call it a weed!—blends well with other flowers in arrangements, or stands alone, feminine and lovely. At summer's end, when the plant goes to seed, it will scatter and re-seed to come back in greater profusion next season.

> *What is a weed? A plant whose virtues*
> *have not yet been discovered.*
> RALPH WALDO EMERSON

THE FRUIT...CONFIDENCE

In today's fast-paced society, everything is moving at an accelerated rate. Competition is fierce. It takes courage to compete, to excel, and to lead.

The confident woman has the assurance that she has prepared well. She is thoroughly certain of her course, yet never cocky. She is a proven leader, yet willing to follow wise counsel. She can be trusted.

This valiant woman can move forward with an inner knowing. She has both won and lost and understands the value of each experience. These life lessons have imparted wisdom and enabled her to see past defeat to victory. The woman of confidence is an inspiration to those who know her.

> *Lives of great men all remind us*
> *We can make our lives sublime;*
> *And, departing, leave behind us*
> *Footprints on the sands of time.*
> HENRY WADSWORTH LONGFELLOW

Woman of Courage...

Margaret Thatcher

As the first female Prime Minister of Great Britain, Margaret Thatcher served the longest term of any British leader—including Winston Churchill. During her 11 years of service, she proved her ability to govern a country as forcefully as any man. Highly intelligent and visionary, she was able to accomplish things that others before her had failed to accomplish—she slashed taxes, reformed the welfare state, and privatized hundreds of industries.

Despite her feminine appearance—she loved high fashion and enjoyed dressing well—Mrs. Thatcher possessed

nerves of steel and the confidence to stand by her convictions. She was often able to push her ideas through the House of Commons. Respected and admired by presidents and kings, she will always be regarded as one of the most outstanding world leaders of all time.

We shall not flag or fail. We shall go on to the end....We shall fight with growing confidence and growing strength....we shall never surrender.
WINSTON CHURCHILL

THE FRAGRANCE

Woman of courage,
dare to dream your dream.
Don't fear society's conventions or the enemies of your soul.
Be true to the inner you. Trust your instincts.
Be confident in the unique design of your life
and trust the One who created it.

CONFIDENCE IS COURAGE.
CONFIDENCE IS INNER PEACE.
CONFIDENCE TACKLES THE IMPOSSIBLE.
CONFIDENCE IS FAITH IN THE FUTURE.

Rose

(ROSACEAE)
LOVE

What's in a name? That which we call a rose
By any other name would smell as sweet.
WILLIAM SHAKESPEARE

THE FLOWER...ROSE

Old-fashioneds, hybrid teas, floribundas, modern shrubs, climbers and ramblers, miniatures—roses come in a wide variety of styles and scents. From the dainty dwarf China rose to the extravagantly full-bloomed cabbage rose, no flower is more beautiful or universally coveted.

Roses are prized for their usefulness as well as their beauty. Historically, roses have been cultivated for their medicinal value; these flowers were thought to relieve headaches, toothaches, even insomnia. The Shakers concocted and sold rose water for its delicate perfume and flavoring. Yet the rose—celebrated by poets and musicians the world over—is perhaps best known as a symbol of love and romance.

If I had a rose for every time
I thought of you,
I'd be picking roses for a lifetime.
SWEDISH QUOTE

THE FRUIT...LOVE

Love is as difficult to define as the mist on the moors or the wind in the trees. It is more often sensed than seen. Love may be heard in a mother's lullaby, a lover's sigh, or a penitent's prayer.

Both a passionate desire and tender compassion, love is a yearning to fill an empty place. Love binds up the brokenhearted and restores lost dreams; it is the glue of life. Love overcomes prejudice and breaks down barriers; it conquers all.

The woman who loves well opens her heart and her home to the unlovable and the unloved. She knows that love brings the power of forgiveness and the promise of new beginnings. She cherishes love's miracle.

When love reigns, the impossible may be attained.
INDIAN PROVERB

Woman of Courage...

Corrie ten Boom

Always kind and hospitable, the ten Boom family in Haarlem, Holland, kept "open house" for anyone in need. But during the turbulent days of World War II, their love for their fellow man took on heroic proportions.

Corrie and her sister, Betsie, along with their father, risked their lives to harbor fugitives hunted down by the Nazis. Hiding these refugees behind a false wall in her bedroom, Corrie spent much of her time caring for their needs or assisting in locating other "safe" houses in the area. Together, she and her neighbors saved the lives of an estimated 800 Jews and protected many others in the Dutch

THE FRAGRANCE

Woman of courage,
to love is to glimpse heaven.
May your love for others be offered freely, sacrificially,
and without condition.
May your scent travel the earth to bless the lives
of those who know not the meaning of love.

underground resistance movement.

Finally arrested and sent to one of the infamous concentration camps near Berlin, Germany, Corrie and Betsie moved among their fellow inmates, sharing the love of God and spreading hope for the future. Despite the tragedy that was going on around her, she was a beautiful rose blooming in strength and courage for the glory of the Lord. When Corrie was released from the death camp, she began a worldwide ministry that took her all over the world—once to a meeting where she encountered the former head of the camp where her beloved sister Betsie had died of malnutrition. But love was greater than hatred, and Corrie was able to forgive him. She passed away on her 91st birthday, considered in Jewish tradition an honor reserved for only very special people.

There is no pit so deep that God's love is not deeper still...He will give us the love to be able to forgive our enemies.
CORRIE TEN BOOM

LOVE IS A MIRACLE.
LOVE IS PATIENT AND KIND.
LOVE IS THE GLUE OF LIFE.
LOVE NEVER FAILS.

Tulip

(LILIACAEA)
DECLARING LOVE

And while the tulip we extol, we'll give the reason why;
'Tis because their varied charms,
As thus they brightly shine,
Remind us of the Almighty hand—
Omnipotence divine!
THE FELTON UNION OF FLORISTS

THE FLOWER...TULIP

The tulip is a flower that has "made men mad." From an Asian wild flower to the highly cultivated worldwide phenomenon it is today, this fabulous flower has charted political history, mirrored economic conditions, and predicted the ebb and flow of religious persecution.

According to a 17th-century garden book, the tulip is "the Queen of bulbous plants, whose flower is beautiful in its figure, and most rich and admirable in color, and wonderful in variety of markings." With all of this infinite variation, the construction of a single tulip is quite simple—six petals and broad green leaves on a slender stem. Yet in Amsterdam, I was once spellbound by the sight of tulip fields too extravagant for the eye!

How could such sweet and wholesome hours
Be reckoned but with herbs and flowers?
ANDREW MARVELL

THE FRUIT...DECLARING LOVE

To declare is to announce, to acknowledge, to make known. Publicly declaring love for another is in itself an act of love.

While we were courting, my husband John signed his letters to me with x's and o's. It was only later that I realized that he was declaring his love. Presenting a beautiful bouquet of flowers—the universal language of love—often serves the same purpose. Since our marriage, John, who loves to grow roses, often sprinkles rose petals on my pillow.

The woman of declaring love will courageously declare her heart's passion. She has tremendous capacity to give as well as receive love. Her love breaks the boundaries of the object of her affection, spills over and becomes a magnet to bless others. Like the magnificent tulip, with its multiplicity of shades and stripes, love may present itself in a variety of ways. "I adore you" is not only spoken by the lips but with the eyes, the heart, and the soul.

How do I love thee? Let me count the ways.
ELIZABETH BARRETT BROWNING

Woman of Courage...
Nancy Reagan

One former president of the United States who would get my vote for declaring love is Ronald Reagan. His love for his wife is legendary. Nancy Reagan recently published a book of love letters, written by her husband to her throughout their marriage.

These public declarations of love are only enhanced by the fact that Mrs. Reagan continues to support her husband, although he is now struggling with the ravages of Alzheimer's and no longer recognizes her. Despite that sad fact, "Ronnie" is still the love of her life.

Nancy Reagan, a woman with a deep capacity for love and unselfish giving, has known hard times before. She displayed courage and stamina in the face of an assassination attempt on her husband in 1981, in the diagnosis of breast cancer in 1987, and in much personal sorrow. But she has held fast to her lifelong belief in the triumph of true love over tragedy.

To have and to hold from this day forward,
for better or for worse, for richer for poorer,
in sickness and in health,
to love and to cherish, till death us do part.
THE BOOK OF COMMON PRAYER

THE FRAGRANCE

Woman of courage,
Boldly declare your love for others.
Don't hide it under a bushel.
Write it down. Shout it out. Send flowers.
Live your legacy of love!

DECLARING LOVE IS PROCLAIMING IT.
DECLARING LOVE IS ANNOUNCING IT.
DECLARING LOVE IS REVEALING IT.
DECLARING LOVE IS LIVING IT.

Violet

(VIOLACEAE)
FAITHFULNESS

I smelt the violets in her hand and asked, half in words,
half in signs, a question which meant, "Is love the
sweetness of flowers?"
HELEN KELLER

THE FLOWER...VIOLET

What a pity flowers can utter no sound!
A singing rose, a whispering violet,
a murmuring honeysuckle—
Oh, what a rare and exquisite miracle would these be!
HENRY WARD BEECHER

Small, shy, and definitely not as showy as other blooms, violets are often overlooked in favor of more flamboyant flowers. The true violet, as its name suggests, is usually found in velvety shades of deep purple or pale lavender.

Most often blooming singly on a stem, seldom in pairs, each bloom is a work of art—gentle and refined. When we think of violets, however, we usually think of "bunches"—a handful of blossoms, arranged in dainty nosegays or in a

small vase. When I think of violets, I recall my
Grandmother Williams, whose favorite color was lavender
and who often wore a bunch of violets pinned to her lapel,
trailing the sweet fragrance behind her like a scented breeze.

THE FRUIT...FAITHFULNESS

Faithfulness is the courage to remain steadfast and
loyal through all circumstances. The faithful woman will be
there in the darkest hour, protecting those she loves with
unyielding dedication. Devoted, dependable, steadfast
relationships are essential to
women of courage.

Never underestimate the
power of two. The power of
two allows for more accountability, more creativity, more
wisdom, and more courage.

*Be faithful until
death, and I will give
you the crown of life.*
THE BOOK OF
REVELATION

Women need other women to impart wisdom,
support and direction to each other. The
woman of faithfulness stands by to give—and
receive—a continuous supply of all that is needed.
She is a life-giver.

Like the violet that whispers rather than
shouts, the faithful woman speaks eloquently
without having to speak loudly. Her essence is the
aroma of faith, hope, and love. The woman of faithfulness covers the hearts of those who trust her.

Women of Courage...

Helen Keller and Anne Sullivan

Two women whose life stories are intertwined with love and faithfulness are Helen Keller and Anne Sullivan. Helen, who was left blind, deaf, and dumb by a devastating childhood illness; and Anne, her lifelong private tutor and faithful friend.

Even in the dark and silent prison cell of her blindness, cut off from the rest of society, little Helen attempted to explore the world using her other senses. She touched and smelled everything. She knew when she was in the garden by the aroma of the flowers and plants and the feel of the ground underfoot.

THE FRAGRANCE

Woman of courage,
may you never be hindered by "impossible" circumstances,
but reach out to achieve the possible.
Like the "whispering violet,"
may the fragrance of faithfulness
so shape the world around you
that it will be a sweeter and better place.

But realizing that she was different presented great problems. Prone to outbursts by her inability to communicate, young Helen was no shrinking violet. She was a handful until the age of seven, when Anne entered her life and began to tame the wild child, giving Helen the tools to overcome her disabilities. Anne taught by touch, using signs to spell out words and sentences in her small student's hand. After learning to speak by feeling the lip and tongue movements of her teacher, Helen went on to master Braille in Greek, Latin, French, and German as well as English.

In 1900 Helen entered Radcliffe College, depending upon her companion to spell out every lecture and examination question. It was through the sacrifice of this faithful teacher, who stood by her for more than fifty years, that Helen Keller was able to impact her culture so profoundly, establishing the American Foundation for the Blind and working to improve conditions for the poverty-stricken and disabled around the world.

FAITHFULNESS IS DEPENDABILITY.
FAITHFULNESS NEVER QUITS.
FAITHFULNESS IS DEVOTION.
FAITHFULNESS IS A FOREVER FRIEND.

Wisteria

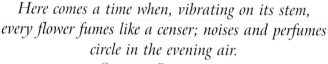

(LEGUMINOSAE)
OBEDIENCE

Here comes a time when, vibrating on its stem,
every flower fumes like a censer; noises and perfumes
circle in the evening air.
CHARLES BAUDELAIRE

THE FLOWER...WISTERIA

This deliciously scented plant is often found spilling over garden walls, arbors, and fences. The small, intricate flowers in shades of mauve, blue, and purple form magnificent clusters, much like grapes, each one cascading from a central stem. A characteristic of the wisteria is its tendency to cling. Tiny green tendrils are sent out to seek a place to hold on, and the vine follows the host, trailing or climbing wherever it leads.

On my wedding day in April, I stepped outside my parents' home and beheld a spectacle I shall never forget. Across the road, where wisteria grows wild, 70-foot tall cypress trees played host to the cascading blossoms, their fragrance sweetening the air for miles around! The vows my new husband and I had just made—"I cling to thee"— seemed to be echoing in the sights and smells of that scene.

Wisteria ties the roof of the porch down;
Morning glory anchors the mailbox;
Green peas keep the garden fence from taking off.
J. B. GOODENOUGH

THE FRUIT...OBEDIENCE

While some perceive obedience as weakness, in fact, quite the opposite is true. A woman who truly understands the meaning of yielding to authority will only grow stronger, wiser, and enjoy great success.

The obedient woman is strong and courageous. Wise enough to know that she does not hold all of life's answers, she defers to those with greater wisdom and experience.

The woman of obedience is twice blessed. By understanding the protocol of life, she will gain great favor and respect, thus, influencing those around her. Like the flower needs the vine, so she needs others and acknowledges the power of clinging and cleaving.

Lives of great men all remind us
We can all make our lives sublime,
And departing, leave behind us
Footprints on the sands of time.
HENRY W. LONGFELLOW

Woman of Courage...

Madame Marie Curie

Marie and Pierre Curie's love story can be told in a few words: obedience to a higher call. The couple first crossed paths when Polish-born Marie moved to Paris to study physics and mathematics at the Sorbonne. She was a brilliant scholar, with a thirst for knowledge; Pierre was already a successful physicist. Their mutual intellectual pursuits soon led to a deeper attraction.

After their marriage they dedicated themselves to science—their chief passion. Obedient to the vision, Marie set out to discover the secrets of uranium, while Pierre

THE FRAGRANCE

Woman of courage,
as you learn to obey, may obedience bring its rewards.
Dare to defy the empty promises of this present age
and find the power in joining hearts and hands.
Your obedience to the vision will bring
a rich and bountiful harvest.

continued his physics research. What they discovered was that two can achieve results more rapidly than one. So Pierre joined Marie in what has become an historic collaboration, literally lighting the darkness with their findings—radium.

This is the true joy in life,
The being used for a purpose recognized
By yourself as a mighty one.
GEORGE BERNARD SHAW

At the ceremony to award the Nobel Prize for Physics to the husband and wife team, the president of the Academy quoted the Book of Genesis: "It is not good that the man should be alone; I will make him an help meet." Marie Curie was not only a helper, but also a leader and is known today as the most outstanding female scientist of all time and a courageous pioneer.

OBEDIENCE TAKES COURAGE.
OBEDIENCE YIELDS TO AUTHORITY.
OBEDIENCE DEMONSTRATES LOYALTY.
OBEDIENCE BRINGS BLESSINGS.

EPILOGUE

Dear Ones,

Charles Dickens once wrote: "It was the best of times, it was the worst of times." Although these words, and many others quoted in this book, were written over a hundred years ago, the truth is as current as today's headlines. These times call for courage.

As you face the future, may you learn the lesson of the flowers. Season after season, they survive, blooming where they are planted or springing up wild and free, under the most difficult of conditions.

Rise up and be strong, Woman of Courage. "If winter comes, can spring be far behind?"

Ann Platz

No winter lasts forever. No spring skips its turn.
HAL BORLAND

CONTACT ME:
1266 West Paces Ferry Road, #521
Atlanta, GA 30327-2306
(website) www.annplatz.com
(e-mail) annplatz@flash.net